This Book Belongs To:

_____

Important Info:

Make: _____

Model: _____

Year Model: _____

Date Acquired: _____

Mileage When Acquired: _____

Oil Type: _____

Oil Capacity: _____

Tire Size: _____

Maximum Tire Pressure: _____

Insurance Company: _____

Insurance Co. Telephone #: _____

Preferred Car Repair Location: _____

AAA Membership #: _____

AAA Contact #: _____

Notes:

Oil Change Record

Date: _____ Mileage:_____

ServiceLocation:_____

Air Filter Changed: Yes No

Cabin Air Filter Changed: Yes No

Wiper Fluid Filled: Yes No

Tire Pressure Checked: Yes No

Other Services Performed:

_____

_____

_____

Other Services Suggested by Service
Technician But Not Completed Today:

_____

_____

Notes:

_____

_____

_____

Next Oil Change Due:

Date: _____ Or

Mileage: _____

Oil Change Record

Date: _____ Mileage:_____

ServiceLocation:_____

Air Filter Changed: Yes   No

Cabin Air Filter Changed: Yes   No

Wiper Fluid Filled: Yes   No

Tire Pressure Checked: Yes   No

Other Services Performed:

_____

_____

_____

Other Services Suggested by Service
Technician But Not Completed Today:

_____

_____

Notes:

_____

_____

_____

Next Oil Change Due:

Date: _____ Or

Mileage: _____

Oil Change Record

Date: _____ Mileage:_____

ServiceLocation:_____

Air Filter Changed: Yes   No

Cabin Air Filter Changed: Yes   No

Wiper Fluid Filled: Yes   No

Tire Pressure Checked: Yes   No

Other Services Performed:

_____

_____

_____

Other Services Suggested by Service
Technician But Not Completed Today:

_____

_____

Notes:

_____

_____

_____

Next Oil Change Due:

Date: _____ Or

Mileage: _____

Oil Change Record

Date: _____ Mileage:_____

ServiceLocation:_____

Air Filter Changed: Yes   No

Cabin Air Filter Changed: Yes   No

Wiper Fluid Filled: Yes   No

Tire Pressure Checked: Yes   No

Other Services Performed:

_____

_____

_____

Other Services Suggested by Service
Technician But Not Completed Today:

_____

_____

Notes:

_____

_____

_____

Next Oil Change Due:

Date: _____ Or

Mileage: _____

Oil Change Record

Date: _____ Mileage:_____

ServiceLocation:_____

Air Filter Changed: Yes   No

Cabin Air Filter Changed: Yes   No

Wiper Fluid Filled: Yes   No

Tire Pressure Checked: Yes   No

Other Services Performed:

_____

_____

_____

Other Services Suggested by Service
Technician But Not Completed Today:

_____

_____

Notes:

_____

_____

_____

Next Oil Change Due:

Date: _____ Or

Mileage: _____

Oil Change Record

Date: _____ Mileage:_____

ServiceLocation:_____

Air Filter Changed: Yes   No

Cabin Air Filter Changed: Yes   No

Wiper Fluid Filled: Yes   No

Tire Pressure Checked: Yes   No

Other Services Performed:

_____
_____
_____

Other Services Suggested by Service
Technician But Not Completed Today:

_____
_____
_____

Notes:
_____
_____
_____

Next Oil Change Due:

Date: _____ Or

Mileage: _____

Oil Change Record

Oil Change Record

Date: _____ Mileage:_____

ServiceLocation:_____

Air Filter Changed: Yes   No

Cabin Air Filter Changed: Yes   No

Wiper Fluid Filled: Yes   No

Tire Pressure Checked: Yes   No

Other Services Performed:

_____

_____

Other Services Suggested by Service
Technician But Not Completed Today:

_____

_____

Notes:

_____

_____

Next Oil Change Due:

Date: _____ Or

Mileage: _____

Oil Change Record

Date: _____ Mileage:_____

ServiceLocation:_____

Air Filter Changed: Yes   No

Cabin Air Filter Changed: Yes   No

Wiper Fluid Filled: Yes   No

Tire Pressure Checked: Yes   No

Other Services Performed:

_____

_____

_____

Other Services Suggested by Service
Technician But Not Completed Today:

_____

_____

Notes:

_____

_____

_____

Next Oil Change Due:

Date: _____ Or

Mileage: _____

Oil Change Record

Oil Change Record

Date: _____ Mileage:_____

ServiceLocation:_____

Air Filter Changed: Yes   No

Cabin Air Filter Changed: Yes   No

Wiper Fluid Filled: Yes   No

Tire Pressure Checked: Yes   No

Other Services Performed:
_____
_____
_____

Other Services Suggested by Service
Technician But Not Completed Today:
_____
_____

Notes:
_____
_____
_____

Next Oil Change Due:

Date: _____ Or

Mileage: _____

Oil Change Record

Date: _____ Mileage:_____

ServiceLocation:_____

Air Filter Changed: Yes   No

Cabin Air Filter Changed: Yes   No

Wiper Fluid Filled: Yes   No

Tire Pressure Checked: Yes   No

Other Services Performed:

_____

_____

_____

Other Services Suggested by Service
Technician But Not Completed Today:

_____

_____

Notes:

_____

_____

_____

Next Oil Change Due:

Date: _____ Or

Mileage: _____

Oil Change Record

Date: _____ Mileage: _____

ServiceLocation: _____

Air Filter Changed: Yes   No

Cabin Air Filter Changed: Yes   No

Wiper Fluid Filled: Yes   No

Tire Pressure Checked: Yes   No

Other Services Performed:

_____

_____

_____

Other Services Suggested by Service
Technician But Not Completed Today:

_____

_____

Notes:

_____

_____

_____

Next Oil Change Due:

Date: _____   Or

Mileage: _____

Oil Change Record

Oil Change Record

Date: _____ Mileage:_____

Service Location:_____

Air Filter Changed: Yes   No

Cabin Air Filter Changed: Yes   No

Wiper Fluid Filled: Yes   No

Tire Pressure Checked: Yes   No

Other Services Performed:

_____

_____

_____

Other Services Suggested by Service
Technician But Not Completed Today:

_____

_____

Notes:

_____

_____

_____

Next Oil Change Due:

Date: _____ Or

Mileage: _____

Oil Change Record

Date: _____ Mileage:_____

ServiceLocation:_____

Air Filter Changed: Yes   No

Cabin Air Filter Changed: Yes   No

Wiper Fluid Filled: Yes   No

Tire Pressure Checked: Yes   No

Other Services Performed:

_____

_____

_____

Other Services Suggested by Service
Technician But Not Completed Today:

_____

_____

Notes:

_____

_____

_____

Next Oil Change Due:

Date: _____ Or

Mileage: _____

Oil Change Record

Date: _____ Mileage:_____

Service Location:_____

Air Filter Changed: Yes   No

Cabin Air Filter Changed: Yes   No

Wiper Fluid Filled: Yes   No

Tire Pressure Checked: Yes   No

Other Services Performed:

_____
_____
_____

Other Services Suggested by Service
Technician But Not Completed Today:

_____
_____

Notes:
_____
_____
_____

Next Oil Change Due:

Date: _____ Or

Mileage: _____

Oil Change Record

Date: _____ Mileage:_____

ServiceLocation:_____

Air Filter Changed: Yes   No

Cabin Air Filter Changed: Yes   No

Wiper Fluid Filled: Yes   No

Tire Pressure Checked: Yes   No

Other Services Performed:

_____

_____

_____

Other Services Suggested by Service
Technician But Not Completed Today:

_____

_____

Notes:

_____

_____

_____

Next Oil Change Due:

Date: _____ Or

Mileage: _____

Oil Change Record

Date: _____ Mileage:_____

ServiceLocation:_____

Air Filter Changed: Yes   No

Cabin Air Filter Changed: Yes   No

Wiper Fluid Filled: Yes   No

Tire Pressure Checked: Yes   No

Other Services Performed:

_____

_____

_____

Other Services Suggested by Service
Technician But Not Completed Today:

_____

_____

Notes:

_____

_____

_____

Next Oil Change Due:

Date: _____ Or

Mileage: _____

Oil Change Record

Date: _____ Mileage: _____

ServiceLocation: _____

Air Filter Changed: Yes   No

Cabin Air Filter Changed: Yes   No

Wiper Fluid Filled: Yes   No

Tire Pressure Checked: Yes   No

Other Services Performed:

_____

_____

Other Services Suggested by Service
Technician But Not Completed Today:

_____

_____

Notes:

_____

_____

Next Oil Change Due:

Date: _____ Or

Mileage: _____

Oil Change Record

Date: _____ Mileage:_____

ServiceLocation:_____

Air Filter Changed: Yes   No

Cabin Air Filter Changed: Yes   No

Wiper Fluid Filled: Yes   No

Tire Pressure Checked: Yes   No

Other Services Performed:

_____

_____

_____

Other Services Suggested by Service
Technician But Not Completed Today:

_____

_____

Notes:

_____

_____

_____

Next Oil Change Due:

Date: _____ Or

Mileage: _____

Oil Change Record

Date: _____ Mileage:_____

ServiceLocation:_____

Air Filter Changed: Yes   No

Cabin Air Filter Changed: Yes   No

Wiper Fluid Filled: Yes   No

Tire Pressure Checked: Yes   No

Other Services Performed:

_____

_____

_____

Other Services Suggested by Service
Technician But Not Completed Today:

_____

_____

Notes:

_____

_____

_____

Next Oil Change Due:

Date: _____ Or

Mileage: _____

Oil Change Record

Date: _____ Mileage:_____

ServiceLocation:_____

Air Filter Changed: Yes   No

Cabin Air Filter Changed: Yes   No

Wiper Fluid Filled: Yes   No

Tire Pressure Checked: Yes   No

Other Services Performed:
_____
_____
_____

Other Services Suggested by Service
Technician But Not Completed Today:
_____
_____

Notes:
_____
_____
_____

Next Oil Change Due:
Date: _____ Or
Mileage: _____

Oil Change Record

Date: _____ Mileage:_____

ServiceLocation:_____

Air Filter Changed: Yes   No

Cabin Air Filter Changed: Yes   No

Wiper Fluid Filled: Yes   No

Tire Pressure Checked: Yes   No

Other Services Performed:

_____

_____

_____

Other Services Suggested by Service
Technician But Not Completed Today:

_____

_____

Notes:

_____

_____

_____

Next Oil Change Due:

Date: _____ Or

Mileage: _____

Oil Change Record

Date: _____ Mileage:_____

Service Location:_____

Air Filter Changed: Yes   No

Cabin Air Filter Changed: Yes   No

Wiper Fluid Filled: Yes   No

Tire Pressure Checked: Yes   No

Other Services Performed:

_____

_____

_____

Other Services Suggested by Service
Technician But Not Completed Today:

_____

_____

Notes:

_____

_____

_____

Next Oil Change Due:

Date: _____ Or

Mileage: _____

Oil Change Record

Date: _____ Mileage:_____

ServiceLocation:_____

Air Filter Changed: Yes   No

Cabin Air Filter Changed: Yes   No

Wiper Fluid Filled: Yes   No

Tire Pressure Checked: Yes   No

Other Services Performed:

_____

_____

_____

Other Services Suggested by Service
Technician But Not Completed Today:

_____

_____

Notes:

_____

_____

_____

Next Oil Change Due:

Date: _____ Or

Mileage: _____

Oil Change Record

Date: _____ Mileage:_____

ServiceLocation:_____

Air Filter Changed: Yes   No

Cabin Air Filter Changed: Yes   No

Wiper Fluid Filled: Yes   No

Tire Pressure Checked: Yes   No

Other Services Performed:

_____

_____

_____

Other Services Suggested by Service
Technician But Not Completed Today:

_____

_____

Notes:
_____

_____

_____

Next Oil Change Due:

Date: _____ Or

Mileage: _____

Oil Change Record

Date: _____ Mileage:_____

ServiceLocation:_____

Air Filter Changed: Yes   No

Cabin Air Filter Changed: Yes   No

Wiper Fluid Filled: Yes   No

Tire Pressure Checked: Yes   No

Other Services Performed:

_____

_____

_____

Other Services Suggested by Service
Technician But Not Completed Today:

_____

_____

Notes:

_____

_____

_____

Next Oil Change Due:

Date: _____ Or

Mileage: _____

Oil Change Record

Date: _____ Mileage:_____

ServiceLocation:_____

Air Filter Changed: Yes   No

Cabin Air Filter Changed: Yes   No

Wiper Fluid Filled: Yes   No

Tire Pressure Checked: Yes   No

Other Services Performed:

_____

_____

_____

Other Services Suggested by Service
Technician But Not Completed Today:

_____

_____

Notes:

_____

_____

_____

Next Oil Change Due:

Date: _____ Or

Mileage: _____

Oil Change Record

Date: _____ Mileage:_____

ServiceLocation:_____

Air Filter Changed: Yes   No

Cabin Air Filter Changed: Yes   No

Wiper Fluid Filled: Yes   No

Tire Pressure Checked: Yes   No

Other Services Performed:

_____

_____

_____

Other Services Suggested by Service
Technician But Not Completed Today:

_____

_____

Notes:

_____

_____

_____

Next Oil Change Due:

Date:_____ Or

Mileage: _____

Oil Change Record

Date: _____ Mileage:_____

Service Location:_____

Air Filter Changed: Yes   No

Cabin Air Filter Changed: Yes   No

Wiper Fluid Filled: Yes   No

Tire Pressure Checked: Yes   No

Other Services Performed:

_____

_____

_____

Other Services Suggested by Service
Technician But Not Completed Today:

_____

_____

Notes:

_____

_____

_____

Next Oil Change Due:

Date: _____ Or

Mileage: _____

Oil Change Record

Oil Change Record

Date: _____ Mileage:_____

ServiceLocation:_____

Air Filter Changed: Yes   No

Cabin Air Filter Changed: Yes   No

Wiper Fluid Filled: Yes   No

Tire Pressure Checked: Yes   No

Other Services Performed:

_____
_____
_____

Other Services Suggested by Service
Technician But Not Completed Today:

_____
_____
_____

Notes:

_____
_____
_____

Next Oil Change Due:

Date: _____ Or

Mileage: _____

Oil Change Record

Date: _____ Mileage: _____

Service Location: _____

Air Filter Changed: Yes   No

Cabin Air Filter Changed: Yes   No

Wiper Fluid Filled: Yes   No

Tire Pressure Checked: Yes   No

Other Services Performed:
_____
_____
_____

Other Services Suggested by Service
Technician But Not Completed Today:
_____
_____

Notes:
_____
_____
_____

Next Oil Change Due:
Date: _____ Or
Mileage: _____

Oil Change Record

Date: _____ Mileage:_____

ServiceLocation:_____

Air Filter Changed: Yes   No

Cabin Air Filter Changed: Yes   No

Wiper Fluid Filled: Yes   No

Tire Pressure Checked: Yes   No

Other Services Performed:

_____

_____

_____

Other Services Suggested by Service
Technician But Not Completed Today:

_____

_____

Notes:

_____

_____

_____

Next Oil Change Due:

Date: _____ Or

Mileage: _____

Oil Change Record

Date: _____ Mileage:_____

ServiceLocation:_____

Air Filter Changed: Yes   No

Cabin Air Filter Changed: Yes   No

Wiper Fluid Filled: Yes   No

Tire Pressure Checked: Yes   No

Other Services Performed:
_____
_____
_____

Other Services Suggested by Service
Technician But Not Completed Today:
_____
_____

Notes:
_____
_____
_____

Next Oil Change Due:

Date: _____ Or

Mileage: _____

Oil Change Record

Date: _____ Mileage:_____

ServiceLocation:_____

Air Filter Changed: Yes   No

Cabin Air Filter Changed: Yes   No

Wiper Fluid Filled: Yes   No

Tire Pressure Checked: Yes   No

Other Services Performed:

_____

_____

_____

Other Services Suggested by Service
Technician But Not Completed Today:

_____

_____

Notes:

_____

_____

_____

Next Oil Change Due:

Date: _____ Or

Mileage: _____

Oil Change Record

Date: _____ Mileage:_____

Service Location:_____

Air Filter Changed: Yes   No

Cabin Air Filter Changed: Yes   No

Wiper Fluid Filled: Yes   No

Tire Pressure Checked: Yes   No

Other Services Performed:

_____

_____

_____

Other Services Suggested by Service
Technician But Not Completed Today:

_____

_____

Notes:

_____

_____

_____

Next Oil Change Due:

Date: _____ Or

Mileage: _____

Oil Change Record

Date: _____ Mileage:_____

ServiceLocation:_____

Air Filter Changed: Yes   No

Cabin Air Filter Changed: Yes   No

Wiper Fluid Filled: Yes   No

Tire Pressure Checked: Yes   No

Other Services Performed:

_____

_____

_____

Other Services Suggested by Service
Technician But Not Completed Today:

_____

_____

Notes:

_____

_____

_____

Next Oil Change Due:

Date: _____ Or

Mileage: _____

Oil Change Record

Date: _____ Mileage:_____

ServiceLocation:_____

Air Filter Changed: Yes   No

Cabin Air Filter Changed: Yes   No

Wiper Fluid Filled: Yes   No

Tire Pressure Checked: Yes   No

Other Services Performed:

_____

_____

_____

Other Services Suggested by Service
Technician But Not Completed Today:

_____

_____

Notes:

_____

_____

_____

Next Oil Change Due:

Date: _____ Or

Mileage:_____

Oil Change Record

Date: _____ Mileage:_____

ServiceLocation:_____

Air Filter Changed: Yes   No

Cabin Air Filter Changed: Yes   No

Wiper Fluid Filled: Yes   No

Tire Pressure Checked: Yes   No

Other Services Performed:

_____

_____

_____

Other Services Suggested by Service
Technician But Not Completed Today:

_____

_____

Notes:

_____

_____

_____

Next Oil Change Due:

Date: _____ Or

Mileage: _____

Oil Change Record

Date: _____ Mileage:_____

ServiceLocation:_____

Air Filter Changed: Yes   No

Cabin Air Filter Changed: Yes   No

Wiper Fluid Filled: Yes   No

Tire Pressure Checked: Yes   No

Other Services Performed:

_____

_____

_____

Other Services Suggested by Service
Technician But Not Completed Today:

_____

_____

Notes:

_____

_____

_____

Next Oil Change Due:

Date: _____ Or

Mileage: _____

Oil Change Record

Date: _____ Mileage:_____

ServiceLocation:_____

Air Filter Changed: Yes   No

Cabin Air Filter Changed: Yes   No

Wiper Fluid Filled: Yes   No

Tire Pressure Checked: Yes   No

Other Services Performed:

_____

_____

_____

Other Services Suggested by Service
Technician But Not Completed Today:

_____

_____

Notes:

_____

_____

_____

Next Oil Change Due:

Date: _____   Or

Mileage: _____

Oil Change Record

Oil Change Record

Date: _____ Mileage:_____

Service Location:_____

Air Filter Changed: Yes   No

Cabin Air Filter Changed: Yes   No

Wiper Fluid Filled: Yes   No

Tire Pressure Checked: Yes   No

Other Services Performed:

_____
_____
_____

Other Services Suggested by Service
Technician But Not Completed Today:

_____
_____

Notes:
_____
_____
_____

Next Oil Change Due:

Date: _____ Or

Mileage: _____

Tire Pressure

Date:_____ Mileage: _____

Tread Depth and Tire Pressure::

Driver's Side: Front - _____Back - _____

Passenger's Side: Front -_____ Back -_____

Date:_____ Mileage: _____

Tread Depth and Tire Pressure::

Driver's Side: Front - _____Back - _____

Passenger's Side: Front -_____ Back -_____

Date:_____ Mileage: _____

Tread Depth and Tire Pressure::

Driver's Side: Front - _____Back - _____

Passenger's Side: Front -_____ Back -_____

Date:_____ Mileage: _____

Tread Depth and Tire Pressure::

Driver's Side: Front - _____Back - _____

Passenger's Side: Front -_____ Back -_____

Tire Pressure

Date:_____ Mileage: _____

Tread Depth and Tire Pressure::

Driver's Side: Front - _____ Back - _____

Passenger's Side: Front -_____ Back -_____

Date:_____ Mileage: _____

Tread Depth and Tire Pressure::

Driver's Side: Front - _____ Back - _____

Passenger's Side: Front -_____ Back -_____

Date:_____ Mileage: _____

Tread Depth and Tire Pressure::

Driver's Side: Front - _____ Back - _____

Passenger's Side: Front -_____ Back -_____

Date:_____ Mileage: _____

Tread Depth and Tire Pressure::

Driver's Side: Front - _____ Back - _____

Passenger's Side: Front -_____ Back -_____

Tire Pressure

Date:_____ Mileage: _____

Tread Depth and Tire Pressure::

Driver's Side: Front - _____ Back - _____

Passenger's Side: Front -_____ Back -_____

Date:_____ Mileage: _____

Tread Depth and Tire Pressure::

Driver's Side: Front - _____ Back - _____

Passenger's Side: Front -_____ Back -_____

Date:_____ Mileage: _____

Tread Depth and Tire Pressure::

Driver's Side: Front - _____ Back - _____

Passenger's Side: Front -_____ Back -_____

Date:_____ Mileage: _____

Tread Depth and Tire Pressure::

Driver's Side: Front - _____ Back - _____

Passenger's Side: Front -_____ Back -_____

Tire Pressure

Date:_____ Mileage: _____

Tread Depth and Tire Pressure::

Driver's Side: Front - _____ Back - _____

Passenger's Side: Front -_____ Back -_____

_____

Date:_____ Mileage: _____

Tread Depth and Tire Pressure::

Driver's Side: Front - _____ Back - _____

Passenger's Side: Front -_____ Back -_____

_____

Date:_____ Mileage: _____

Tread Depth and Tire Pressure::

Driver's Side: Front - _____ Back - _____

Passenger's Side: Front -_____ Back -_____

_____

Date:_____ Mileage: _____

Tread Depth and Tire Pressure::

Driver's Side: Front - _____ Back - _____

Passenger's Side: Front -_____ Back -_____

_____

Tire Pressure

Date:_____ Mileage: _____

Tread Depth and Tire Pressure::

Driver's Side: Front - _____ Back - _____

Passenger's Side: Front -_____ Back -_____

Date:_____ Mileage: _____

Tread Depth and Tire Pressure::

Driver's Side: Front - _____ Back - _____

Passenger's Side: Front -_____ Back -_____

Date:_____ Mileage: _____

Tread Depth and Tire Pressure::

Driver's Side: Front - _____ Back - _____

Passenger's Side: Front -_____ Back -_____

Date:_____ Mileage: _____

Tread Depth and Tire Pressure::

Driver's Side: Front - _____ Back - _____

Passenger's Side: Front -_____ Back -_____

Tire Pressure

Date:_____ Mileage: _____

Tread Depth and Tire Pressure::

Driver's Side: Front - _____ Back - _____

Passenger's Side: Front -_____ Back -_____

Date:_____ Mileage: _____

Tread Depth and Tire Pressure::

Driver's Side: Front - _____ Back - _____

Passenger's Side: Front -_____ Back -_____

Date:_____ Mileage: _____

Tread Depth and Tire Pressure::

Driver's Side: Front - _____ Back - _____

Passenger's Side: Front -_____ Back -_____

Date:_____ Mileage: _____

Tread Depth and Tire Pressure::

Driver's Side: Front - _____ Back - _____

Passenger's Side: Front -_____ Back -_____

Tire Pressure

Date:_____ Mileage: _____

Tread Depth and Tire Pressure::

Driver's Side: Front - _____Back - _____

Passenger's Side: Front -_____ Back -_____

Date:_____ Mileage: _____

Tread Depth and Tire Pressure::

Driver's Side: Front - _____Back - _____

Passenger's Side: Front -_____ Back -_____

Date:_____ Mileage: _____

Tread Depth and Tire Pressure::

Driver's Side: Front - _____Back - _____

Passenger's Side: Front -_____ Back -_____

Date:_____ Mileage: _____

Tread Depth and Tire Pressure::

Driver's Side: Front - _____Back - _____

Passenger's Side: Front -_____ Back -_____

Tire Pressure

Date:_____ Mileage: _____

Tread Depth and Tire Pressure::

Driver's Side: Front - _____ Back - _____

Passenger's Side: Front -_____ Back -_____

Date:_____ Mileage: _____

Tread Depth and Tire Pressure::

Driver's Side: Front - _____ Back - _____

Passenger's Side: Front -_____ Back -_____

Date:_____ Mileage: _____

Tread Depth and Tire Pressure::

Driver's Side: Front - _____ Back - _____

Passenger's Side: Front -_____ Back -_____

Date:_____ Mileage: _____

Tread Depth and Tire Pressure::

Driver's Side: Front - _____ Back - _____

Passenger's Side: Front -_____ Back -_____

Tire Pressure

Date:_____ Mileage: _____

Tread Depth and Tire Pressure::

Driver's Side: Front - _____ Back - _____

Passenger's Side: Front -_____ Back -_____

Date:_____ Mileage: _____

Tread Depth and Tire Pressure::

Driver's Side: Front - _____ Back - _____

Passenger's Side: Front -_____ Back -_____

Date:_____ Mileage: _____

Tread Depth and Tire Pressure::

Driver's Side: Front - _____ Back - _____

Passenger's Side: Front -_____ Back -_____

Date:_____ Mileage: _____

Tread Depth and Tire Pressure::

Driver's Side: Front - _____ Back - _____

Passenger's Side: Front -_____ Back -_____

Tire Pressure

Date:_____ Mileage: _____

Tread Depth and Tire Pressure::

Driver's Side: Front - _____ Back - _____

Passenger's Side: Front -_____ Back -_____

Date:_____ Mileage: _____

Tread Depth and Tire Pressure::

Driver's Side: Front - _____ Back - _____

Passenger's Side: Front -_____ Back -_____

Date:_____ Mileage: _____

Tread Depth and Tire Pressure::

Driver's Side: Front - _____ Back - _____

Passenger's Side: Front -_____ Back -_____

Date:_____ Mileage: _____

Tread Depth and Tire Pressure::

Driver's Side: Front - _____ Back - _____

Passenger's Side: Front -_____ Back -_____

Tire Pressure

Tire Pressure

Date:_____ Mileage: _____

Tread Depth and Tire Pressure::

Driver's Side: Front - _____ Back - _____

Passenger's Side: Front -_____ Back -_____

Date:_____ Mileage: _____

Tread Depth and Tire Pressure::

Driver's Side: Front - _____ Back - _____

Passenger's Side: Front -_____ Back -_____

Date:_____ Mileage: _____

Tread Depth and Tire Pressure::

Driver's Side: Front - _____ Back - _____

Passenger's Side: Front -_____ Back -_____

Date:_____ Mileage: _____

Tread Depth and Tire Pressure::

Driver's Side: Front - _____ Back - _____

Passenger's Side: Front -_____ Back -_____

Tire Pressure

Date:_____ Mileage: _____

Tread Depth and Tire Pressure::

Driver's Side: Front - _____ Back - _____

Passenger's Side: Front -_____ Back -_____

Date:_____ Mileage: _____

Tread Depth and Tire Pressure::

Driver's Side: Front - _____ Back - _____

Passenger's Side: Front -_____ Back -_____

Date:_____ Mileage: _____

Tread Depth and Tire Pressure::

Driver's Side: Front - _____ Back - _____

Passenger's Side: Front -_____ Back -_____

Date:_____ Mileage: _____

Tread Depth and Tire Pressure::

Driver's Side: Front - _____ Back - _____

Passenger's Side: Front -_____ Back -_____

Tire Pressure

Tire Pressure

Date:_____ Mileage: _____

Tread Depth and Tire Pressure::

Driver's Side: Front - _____ Back - _____

Passenger's Side: Front -_____ Back -_____

Date:_____ Mileage: _____

Tread Depth and Tire Pressure::

Driver's Side: Front - _____ Back - _____

Passenger's Side: Front -_____ Back -_____

Date:_____ Mileage: _____

Tread Depth and Tire Pressure::

Driver's Side: Front - _____ Back - _____

Passenger's Side: Front -_____ Back -_____

Date:_____ Mileage: _____

Tread Depth and Tire Pressure::

Driver's Side: Front - _____ Back - _____

Passenger's Side: Front -_____ Back -_____

Tire Pressure

Tire Pressure

Date:_____ Mileage: _____

Tread Depth and Tire Pressure::

Driver's Side: Front - _____ Back - _____

Passenger's Side: Front -_____ Back -_____

Date:_____ Mileage: _____

Tread Depth and Tire Pressure::

Driver's Side: Front - _____ Back - _____

Passenger's Side: Front -_____ Back -_____

Date:_____ Mileage: _____

Tread Depth and Tire Pressure::

Driver's Side: Front - _____ Back - _____

Passenger's Side: Front -_____ Back -_____

Date:_____ Mileage: _____

Tread Depth and Tire Pressure::

Driver's Side: Front - _____ Back - _____

Passenger's Side: Front -_____ Back -_____

Tire Pressure

Date:_____ Mileage: _____

Tread Depth and Tire Pressure::

Driver's Side: Front - _____ Back - _____

Passenger's Side: Front -_____ Back -_____

Date:_____ Mileage: _____

Tread Depth and Tire Pressure::

Driver's Side: Front - _____ Back - _____

Passenger's Side: Front -_____ Back -_____

Date:_____ Mileage: _____

Tread Depth and Tire Pressure::

Driver's Side: Front - _____ Back - _____

Passenger's Side: Front -_____ Back -_____

Date:_____ Mileage: _____

Tread Depth and Tire Pressure::

Driver's Side: Front - _____ Back - _____

Passenger's Side: Front -_____ Back -_____

Tire Pressure

Date:_____ Mileage: _____

Tread Depth and Tire Pressure::

Driver's Side: Front - _____ Back - _____

Passenger's Side: Front -_____ Back -_____

Date:_____ Mileage: _____

Tread Depth and Tire Pressure::

Driver's Side: Front - _____ Back - _____

Passenger's Side: Front -_____ Back -_____

Date:_____ Mileage: _____

Tread Depth and Tire Pressure::

Driver's Side: Front - _____ Back - _____

Passenger's Side: Front -_____ Back -_____

Date:_____ Mileage: _____

Tread Depth and Tire Pressure::

Driver's Side: Front - _____ Back - _____

Passenger's Side: Front -_____ Back -_____

Tire Pressure

Date:_____ Mileage: _____

Tread Depth and Tire Pressure::

Driver's Side: Front - _____ Back - _____

Passenger's Side: Front -_____ Back -_____

Date:_____ Mileage: _____

Tread Depth and Tire Pressure::

Driver's Side: Front - _____ Back - _____

Passenger's Side: Front -_____ Back -_____

Date:_____ Mileage: _____

Tread Depth and Tire Pressure::

Driver's Side: Front - _____ Back - _____

Passenger's Side: Front -_____ Back -_____

Date:_____ Mileage: _____

Tread Depth and Tire Pressure::

Driver's Side: Front - _____ Back - _____

Passenger's Side: Front -_____ Back -_____

Tire Pressure

Date:_____ Mileage: _____

Tread Depth and Tire Pressure::

Driver's Side: Front - _____ Back - _____

Passenger's Side: Front -_____ Back -_____

Date:_____ Mileage: _____

Tread Depth and Tire Pressure::

Driver's Side: Front - _____ Back - _____

Passenger's Side: Front -_____ Back -_____

Date:_____ Mileage: _____

Tread Depth and Tire Pressure::

Driver's Side: Front - _____ Back - _____

Passenger's Side: Front -_____ Back -_____

Date:_____ Mileage: _____

Tread Depth and Tire Pressure::

Driver's Side: Front - _____ Back - _____

Passenger's Side: Front -_____ Back -_____

Tire Pressure

Date:_____ Mileage: _____

Tread Depth and Tire Pressure::

Driver's Side: Front - _____ Back - _____

Passenger's Side: Front -_____ Back -_____

Date:_____ Mileage: _____

Tread Depth and Tire Pressure::

Driver's Side: Front - _____ Back - _____

Passenger's Side: Front -_____ Back -_____

Date:_____ Mileage: _____

Tread Depth and Tire Pressure::

Driver's Side: Front - _____ Back - _____

Passenger's Side: Front -_____ Back -_____

Date:_____ Mileage: _____

Tread Depth and Tire Pressure::

Driver's Side: Front - _____ Back - _____

Passenger's Side: Front -_____ Back -_____

Tire Pressure

Date:_____ Mileage: _____

Tread Depth and Tire Pressure::

Driver's Side: Front - _____ Back - _____

Passenger's Side: Front -_____ Back -_____

Date:_____ Mileage: _____

Tread Depth and Tire Pressure::

Driver's Side: Front - _____ Back - _____

Passenger's Side: Front -_____ Back -_____

Date:_____ Mileage: _____

Tread Depth and Tire Pressure::

Driver's Side: Front - _____ Back - _____

Passenger's Side: Front -_____ Back -_____

Date:_____ Mileage: _____

Tread Depth and Tire Pressure::

Driver's Side: Front - _____ Back - _____

Passenger's Side: Front -_____ Back -_____

Tire Replacement

Date: _____ Mileage: _____

Brand of Tire: _____

Replaced All Tires? Yes   No

If No, Which Tires Were Replaced: _____

_____

Where Were Tires Purchased? _____

Cost Per Tire: _____

Warranty Information: _____

_____

Notes: _____

_____

_____

Date: _____ Mileage: _____

Brand of Tire: _____

Replaced All Tires? Yes   No

If No, Which Tires Were Replaced: _____

_____

Where Were Tires Purchased? _____

Cost Per Tire: _____

Warranty Information: _____

_____

Notes: _____

_____

_____

Tire Replacement

Date: _____ Mileage: _____

Brand of Tire: _____

Replaced All Tires? Yes   No

If No, Which Tires Were Replaced: _____
_____

Where Were Tires Purchased? _____

Cost Per Tire: _____

Warranty Information: _____
_____

Notes: _____
_____
_____

Date: _____ Mileage: _____

Brand of Tire: _____

Replaced All Tires? Yes   No

If No, Which Tires Were Replaced: _____
_____

Where Were Tires Purchased? _____

Cost Per Tire: _____

Warranty Information: _____
_____

Notes: _____
_____
_____

Tire Replacement

Date: _____ Mileage: _____

Brand of Tire: _____

Replaced All Tires? Yes   No

If No, Which Tires Were Replaced: _____

_____

Where Were Tires Purchased? _____

Cost Per Tire: _____

Warranty Information: _____

_____

Notes: _____

_____

_____

Date: _____ Mileage: _____

Brand of Tire: _____

Replaced All Tires? Yes   No

If No, Which Tires Were Replaced: _____

_____

Where Were Tires Purchased? _____

Cost Per Tire: _____

Warranty Information: _____

_____

Notes: _____

_____

_____

Tire Replacement

Date: _____ Mileage: _____

Brand of Tire: _____

Replaced All Tires? Yes   No

If No, Which Tires Were Replaced: _____
_____

Where Were Tires Purchased? _____

Cost Per Tire: _____

Warranty Information: _____
_____

Notes: _____
_____
_____

Date: _____ Mileage: _____

Brand of Tire: _____

Replaced All Tires? Yes   No

If No, Which Tires Were Replaced: _____
_____

Where Were Tires Purchased? _____

Cost Per Tire: _____

Warranty Information: _____
_____

Notes: _____
_____
_____

Service, Maintenance or Repair Record

Date: _____ Mileage: _____

Type of Service: _____

Service Location: _____

Cost: _____

Covered by Insurance? Yes   No

Notes: _____

_____

_____

_____

_____

_____

_____

Date: _____ Mileage: _____

Type of Service: _____

Service Location: _____

Cost: _____

Covered by Insurance? Yes   No

Notes: _____

_____

_____

_____

_____

_____

_____

Service, Maintenance or Repair Record

Date: _____ Mileage: _____

Type of Service: _____

Service Location: _____

Cost: _____

Covered by Insurance? Yes   No

Notes: _____

_____

_____

_____

_____

_____

_____

Date: _____ Mileage: _____

Type of Service: _____

Service Location: _____

Cost: _____

Covered by Insurance? Yes   No

Notes: _____

_____

_____

_____

_____

_____

_____

Service, Maintenance or Repair Record

Date: _____ Mileage: _____

Type of Service: _____

Service Location: _____

Cost: _____

Covered by Insurance? Yes   No

Notes: _____

_____

_____

_____

_____

_____

_____

Date: _____ Mileage: _____

Type of Service: _____

Service Location: _____

Cost: _____

Covered by Insurance? Yes   No

Notes: _____

_____

_____

_____

_____

_____

_____

Service, Maintenance or Repair Record

Date: _____ Mileage: _____

Type of Service: _____

Service Location: _____

Cost: _____

Covered by Insurance? Yes   No

Notes: _____
_____
_____
_____
_____
_____
_____

Date: _____ Mileage: _____

Type of Service: _____

Service Location: _____

Cost: _____

Covered by Insurance? Yes   No

Notes: _____
_____
_____
_____
_____
_____
_____

Service, Maintenance or Repair Record

Date: _____ Mileage: _____

Type of Service: _____

Service Location: _____

Cost: _____

Covered by Insurance? Yes   No

Notes: _____
_____
_____
_____
_____
_____
_____

Date: _____ Mileage: _____

Type of Service: _____

Service Location: _____

Cost: _____

Covered by Insurance? Yes   No

Notes: _____
_____
_____
_____
_____
_____
_____

Service, Maintenance or Repair Record

Date: _____ Mileage: _____

Type of Service: _____

Service Location: _____

Cost: _____

Covered by Insurance? Yes   No

Notes: _____

_____

_____

_____

_____

_____

_____

Date: _____ Mileage: _____

Type of Service: _____

Service Location: _____

Cost: _____

Covered by Insurance? Yes   No

Notes: _____

_____

_____

_____

_____

_____

_____

Service, Maintenance or Repair Record

Date: _____ Mileage: _____

Type of Service: _____

Service Location: _____

Cost: _____

Covered by Insurance? Yes   No

Notes: _____

_____

_____

_____

_____

_____

_____

Date: _____ Mileage: _____

Type of Service: _____

Service Location: _____

Cost: _____

Covered by Insurance? Yes   No

Notes: _____

_____

_____

_____

_____

_____

_____

Service, Maintenance or Repair Record

Date: _____ Mileage: _____

Type of Service: _____

Service Location: _____

Cost: _____

Covered by Insurance? Yes   No

Notes: _____

_____

_____

_____

_____

_____

_____

Date: _____ Mileage: _____

Type of Service: _____

Service Location: _____

Cost: _____

Covered by Insurance? Yes   No

Notes: _____

_____

_____

_____

_____

_____

_____

Service, Maintenance or Repair Record

Date: _____ Mileage: _____

Type of Service: _____

Service Location: _____

Cost: _____

Covered by Insurance? Yes   No

Notes: _____

_____

_____

_____

_____

_____

_____

Date: _____ Mileage: _____

Type of Service: _____

Service Location: _____

Cost: _____

Covered by Insurance? Yes   No

Notes: _____

_____

_____

_____

_____

_____

_____

Service, Maintenance or Repair Record

Date: _____ Mileage: _____

Type of Service: _____

Service Location: _____

Cost: _____

Covered by Insurance? Yes   No

Notes: _____

_____

_____

_____

_____

_____

_____

Date: _____ Mileage: _____

Type of Service: _____

Service Location: _____

Cost: _____

Covered by Insurance? Yes   No

Notes: _____

_____

_____

_____

_____

_____

_____

Service, Maintenance or Repair Record

Date: _____ Mileage: _____

Type of Service: _____

Service Location: _____

Cost: _____

Covered by Insurance? Yes   No

Notes: _____

_____

_____

_____

_____

_____

_____

Date: _____ Mileage: _____

Type of Service: _____

Service Location: _____

Cost: _____

Covered by Insurance? Yes   No

Notes: _____

_____

_____

_____

_____

_____

_____

Service, Maintenance or Repair Record

Date: _____ Mileage: _____

Type of Service: _____

Service Location: _____

Cost: _____

Covered by Insurance? Yes   No

Notes: _____

_____

_____

_____

_____

_____

_____

Date: _____ Mileage: _____

Type of Service: _____

Service Location: _____

Cost: _____

Covered by Insurance? Yes   No

Notes: _____

_____

_____

_____

_____

_____

_____

Service, Maintenance or Repair Record

Date: _____ Mileage: _____

Type of Service: _____

Service Location: _____

Cost: _____

Covered by Insurance? Yes   No

Notes: _____

_____

_____

_____

_____

_____

_____

Date: _____ Mileage: _____

Type of Service: _____

Service Location: _____

Cost: _____

Covered by Insurance? Yes   No

Notes: _____

_____

_____

_____

_____

_____

_____

Service, Maintenance or Repair Record

Date: _____ Mileage: _____

Type of Service: _____

Service Location: _____

Cost: _____

Covered by Insurance? Yes   No

Notes: _____

_____

_____

_____

_____

_____

_____

Date: _____ Mileage: _____

Type of Service: _____

Service Location: _____

Cost: _____

Covered by Insurance? Yes   No

Notes: _____

_____

_____

_____

_____

_____

_____

Service, Maintenance or Repair Record

Date: _____ Mileage: _____

Type of Service: _____

Service Location: _____

Cost: _____

Covered by Insurance? Yes   No

Notes: _____
_____
_____
_____
_____
_____
_____

Date: _____ Mileage: _____

Type of Service: _____

Service Location: _____

Cost: _____

Covered by Insurance? Yes   No

Notes: _____
_____
_____
_____
_____
_____

Service, Maintenance or Repair Record

Date: _____ Mileage: _____

Type of Service: _____

Service Location: _____

Cost: _____

Covered by Insurance? Yes   No

Notes: _____

_____

_____

_____

_____

_____

_____

Date: _____ Mileage: _____

Type of Service: _____

Service Location: _____

Cost: _____

Covered by Insurance? Yes   No

Notes: _____

_____

_____

_____

_____

_____

_____

Service, Maintenance or Repair Record

Date: _____ Mileage: _____

Type of Service: _____

Service Location: _____

Cost: _____

Covered by Insurance? Yes   No

Notes: _____

_____

_____

_____

_____

_____

_____

Date: _____ Mileage: _____

Type of Service: _____

Service Location: _____

Cost: _____

Covered by Insurance? Yes   No

Notes: _____

_____

_____

_____

_____

_____

_____

Service, Maintenance or Repair Record

Date: _____ Mileage: _____

Type of Service: _____

Service Location: _____

Cost: _____

Covered by Insurance? Yes   No

Notes: _____

_____

_____

_____

_____

_____

_____

Date: _____ Mileage: _____

Type of Service: _____

Service Location: _____

Cost: _____

Covered by Insurance? Yes   No

Notes: _____

_____

_____

_____

_____

_____

_____

Service, Maintenance or Repair Record

Date: _____ Mileage: _____

Type of Service: _____

Service Location: _____

Cost: _____

Covered by Insurance? Yes   No

Notes: _____

_____

_____

_____

_____

_____

_____

Date: _____ Mileage: _____

Type of Service: _____

Service Location: _____

Cost: _____

Covered by Insurance? Yes   No

Notes: _____

_____

_____

_____

_____

_____

_____

Service, Maintenance or Repair Record

Date: _____ Mileage: _____

Type of Service: _____

Service Location: _____

Cost: _____

Covered by Insurance? Yes   No

Notes: _____

_____

_____

_____

_____

_____

_____

Date: _____ Mileage: _____

Type of Service: _____

Service Location: _____

Cost: _____

Covered by Insurance? Yes   No

Notes: _____

_____

_____

_____

_____

_____

_____

Trip Log

Date: From: To: Purpose: Odo. Reading: Miles Traveled:

Trip Log

Trip Log

Date:	From:	To:	Purpose:	Odo. Reading:	Miles Traveled:

Trip Log

Trip Log

Date:	From:	To:	Purpose:	Odo. Reading:	Miles Traveled:

Trip Log

Trip Log

Date:	From:	To:	Purpose:	Odo. Reading:	Miles Traveled:

Trip Log

Trip Log

Date:	From:	To:	Purpose:	Odo. Reading:	Miles Traveled:

Trip Log

Trip Log

Date: From: To: Purpose: Odo. Reading: Miles Traveled:

Trip Log

Trip Log

Date: From: To: Purpose: Odo. Reading: Miles Traveled:

Trip Log

Date:	From:	To:	Purpose:	Odo. Reading:	Miles Traveled:

Trip Log

Gas Mileage Log

Date:	Curr. Odo. Reading:	Prev. Odo. Reading:	Miles Traveled:	Gallons Added:	Miles Traveled/ Gallons Added = MPG

Gas Mileage Log

Gas Mileage Log

Date:	Curr. Odo. Reading:	Prev. Odo. Reading:	Miles Traveled:	Gallons Added:	Miles Traveled/ Gallons Added = MPG

Gas Mileage Log

Date:	Curr. Odo. Reading:	Prev. Odo. Reading:	Miles Traveled:	Gallons Added:	Miles Traveled/ Gallons Added = MPG

Gas Mileage Log

Date:	Curr. Odo. Reading:	Prev. Odo. Reading:	Miles Traveled:	Gallons Added:	Miles Traveled/ Gallons Added = MPG

Gas Mileage Log

Date:	Curr. Odo. Reading:	Prev. Odo. Reading:	Miles Traveled:	Gallons Added:	Miles Traveled/ Gallons Added = MPG

Gas Mileage Log

Date:	Curr. Odo. Reading:	Prev. Odo. Reading:	Miles Traveled:	Gallons Added:	Miles Traveled/ Gallons Added = MPG

Gas Mileage Log

Date:	Curr. Odo. Reading:	Prev. Odo. Reading:	Miles Traveled:	Gallons Added:	Miles Traveled/ Gallons Added = MPG

Gas Mileage Log

Date:	Curr. Odo. Reading:	Prev. Odo. Reading:	Miles Traveled:	Gallons Added:	Miles Traveled/ Gallons Added = MPG

Gas Mileage Log

Notes:

Notes:

Made in the USA
Las Vegas, NV
13 January 2024

84342058R00059